Disorganized Thoughts

ISBN: 9798666354292

Printed in the United States of America

Acknowledgement

I would like to thank my wife, kids, parents, siblings, and many friends who have inspired and provided the beautiful experiences I have witnessed so far in my life. They also gave me the encouragement, whether openly or silently, to put this book together, even though I told only my wife, I was writing this book. However, I know my family and friends, so if I told them I was doing it, they would have provided me, the words of encouragement to write it. I do thank and love you all!!!

Special Thanks goes to John and Sharon E.(inspiration). My wife J.A.M for putting up with me.

Introduction

Disorganized thoughts? So how did I come up with such a name? Let's just say I am writing this amid global pandemic, where elected leaders across the globe have to make some critical decisions if they're lucky in a matter of hours, that will have a rippling effect across the country they lead. And the crazy thing is, no matter what decision they make, it will not make 100% of the people happy. Whatever decision is made, some will agree, while others will oppose it. Now, this is our planet, and no matter what country you choose to visit, trust and believe this is just one out of the thousands, and depending on your country, it could be one out of the millions, of issues that a president and their governments are facing. You look at television or read the news, for those of us that still read, all you hear and see is a lot of negativity. Think about it, even reality television is built around competition and controversy. So how did we get here? A planet where competition, debate, and negativity are how you truly make a living. So, what do we expect? This book was not prewritten or some journal or diary of notes that I decided to put together. I am

writing this book as I go.

My mind is in an ongoing race against who knows what. But with so much going on

today, I decided to put these thoughts in a book, as they come to me, over the course of one

day. Exactly, this book will be completed in a day. As we journey, you will see how

disorganized my mind is, yet there is the logic behind it, or my logic at least. I can assure

you, that I will touch on some pretty touchy subjects. Subjects I do not discuss with most

family members and I would not dare to have these conversations with a stranger. I created

this short book, as there is so much to do these days, other than reading, but I do hope you

will complete this brief journey through my mind. Then, in the end, I may share a bit of

what I think and how I navigate through this crazy world. I will warn you now, the

opinions in here are merely my own, if we think alike on some things or even all things,

well I look forward to crossing paths with you and if you don't agree with anything, well I

look forward to crossing paths with you also.

Nothing in this book is fact. This book is the thoughts inside of the mind of a person with tremendous anxiety. Anxiety, from what I am witnessing and experiencing currently and, from what I have experienced in the past, while navigating through this thing called life.

Warning: This book is quite disorganized, so do not judge me on my organizational format. Now, sit back, get comfortable, and hopefully, this ride inside my mind will be enjoyable and maybe help create some dialogue in the future.

Buckle Up

Since there is no format, there is no actual beginning to this second of three chapters, so I will start with my take on how we got here today, in a general form. If you ask most astrologist how old earth is, most will say millions, trillions, or zillions of years old. Most religious leaders have it somewhere in the thousands, I would guess, depending on the religion and those with actual scripts or texts written during those times. Either way, no one can say how old the planet is precisely, but it is here, and we live on it. I think through time and evolution or from existence, whichever, there were two beings with the ability to reproduce of course and they would be our ancestral parents of everyone here today.

As population grew, people migrated, and before you know it, various areas became populated. In these separate areas, the different groups created their very own distinct identity, language, and over time these distinct groups became friends and/or enemies of other groups. With that thought alone, my mind has changed its thought process, because,

throughout the centuries, the theme has been about differences, division, exclusion and/or

conquer. The line of division or shall I say the line between them and us has grown

tremendously, and I believe that is the root of all the madness we see and experience

today. How many times can you take a planet, a religion, a race, a country, a group, a

family, a person and divide them? That is how we have gotten here. We have divided the

planet and the people so much that it is going to take sure will and determination from

everyone to bring us back together. And that would mean having to drop all the labels and

affiliations to practically everything you identify yourself as or to. See, that is a lot harder

than it sounds.

Politics

Let us start with politics because the last story I read, before writing was about politics. Do not worry about the story but let us discuss politics. I will use the United States political system in this example, but you can plug and play with this because it is the central concept of politics in most countries. Now, this is one of two subjects I do not talk about in a group, with a stranger or even with family. There is really only one person I will speak on this subject with and we usually get on the subject about once a month, but that is it. As I put out my thoughts on the matter, I will tread lightly, as this is a subject that people take pretty seriously. I will start by saying as an individual and a parent, I teach my kids to be themselves and have their own minds. I tell them it is okay to follow the group sometime if they are doing something right or lead the group sometimes, but the main thing is to be an individual and do it because you want to and not because everyone else is doing it. Then they grow, and when it comes to politics in most countries, you have to choose a side, even if you do not 100% agree with everything that side agrees with or the candidates that your

side offers.

Today, politics is done as a group and with group politics, they move and vote as a unit.

Kind of like a gang, for those I may have lost with my last statement talking about groups

also called parties. I guess they could be considered a little nicer than most gangs, I guess,

but still all the same, they have helped people, and they have hurt people. They have turf

wars called battleground states, then they have their home states, basically states they pretty

much know they will win. Before I go in on politics, let me say any politician, it does not

matter what country, but anyone who holds or have held a position or an office, hats off to

you because that is one job I would prefer not to do or run for. I thought about it once, but

my dad busted that bubble quick, because he said I would change as a person, if I got into

politics and he was probably right. There is too much money involved with politics and

you must do something to get that money. I have not met anyone who just gave a lot of

money to someone for nothing. However, as a politician how can you vote as an individual

when you are a part of a group. If you vote against the group and get a reputation for going against the group, you risk getting kicked out of the group or being put on some smaller level committee. Even if, deep inside you, you want to go against what the group thinks because as an individual that is how you feel, but you stick with the group anyway so you do not receive any backlash. So, here is my first disagreement with politics. I honestly could go on to the next topic.

We are brought up and taught to be an individual, yet we are being governed by a bunch of individuals that think and act as a group. Now in society, each individual either goes with the group their parents are a part of, or they vote with the group that votes for or against whichever legislations that is near and dear to them. I am sure most people can find something their group was for or against that they did not agree with, but as long as they vote in favor of the things that matter to them, you will have their vote. Think about the ads, this candidate is soft on guns and wants to take your guns away. NEWS FLASH PEOPLE, no one can or will take your guns away, yet people buy into the fear.

Random Thought

In my honest opinion, no one person or group should have enough weapons to outgun the police force or military. To me, that's a problem, but the other problem is the fact that most of the guns used in street crimes or gang activities are illegal, so it would not matter what legislation you pass, it will not stop people from purchasing guns or the guns they want. So, you may want to use some of the resources and find out where all these illegal guns are coming from or find the illegal gun factory that is making the guns. Most people are not going to back gun reform, when there are some people in the population that can get guns with a reform or not. Now that's the truth. The various agencies can hunt someone down and punish them for unpaid taxes, parking tickets or missing court, but hundreds, thousands, could be millions of illegal guns are on the streets and no one knows where they come from. Somebody has to knows something; I'm just not buying it. And really you can do this with any issue no matter the party, whether its criminal justice reform or war on drugs, you name it. It is fear that is put in place to draw voters to their party. Sorry, mind

racing, back to politics.

Back to Politics

I think the two-party system was created by design, because most people don't have the time to listen or read up on every single candidate that is going to be on a ballet, it is much easier to go in and cast your vote for the group, like they call it, a straight ticket. Then again, it is not that hard, but how many people really want to take the time, to listen to each candidate that is going to be on the ticket. Now there is one reason for joining one of the gangs, sorry I meant parties, it makes voting easier and a lot faster. However, to me at least, a nicer and more comforting idea, would be if those running or holding the office of president would have to drop their party affiliation. I think the separate parties should agree on a baseline budget that they feel is sufficient to run for office and the parties cover evenly what the candidates are unable to raise through fundraisers. Either way or however they figure it out, I do not think the president should be tied to a political party. I feel the president should be the most unbiased person in office because they're holding a position that affects so many. Lose the party affiliation and run on what you really believe, that is how it should be.

Random Thought

Apologies, but I had another random thought come to mind and I felt the need to add it as soon as it popped. In the United States, there are and have been problems with the police and their treatment to people of color. Before I start, let me say I tip my hat to all the good cops out there because that is another job I would not like to have or even consider doing. Now, police chiefs, police unions heads, governors, mayors, and other politicians, I am not quite sure why no one seems to have a solution for this because without a solution, it seems like nothing will change. Are they expecting the latest incident to be the final incident? Or is everyone looking at the next person to figure it out? There is only one way solve it and that is with legislation that changes the rules of engagement for law enforcement.

Rules of engagement for those of you that do not know, is basically what has to happen or circumstances in order for a solider to fire their weapon at someone in a warzone or period. Most people do not know, but U.S. soldiers fighting in a warzone have tougher rules of engagement than police officers in the United States. This could be a rumor, just saying, but I heard it takes an act of congress or at least orders from a commanding officer, in order for your average solider to engage or fire their weapon at someone. I am not talking about your black ops' personnel, but most of the regular soldiers that are in theater. So, rule number one should be no one fires their gun unless they see the suspect with a gun. Let us be reasonable, if the suspect is carrying a weapon that is visible and especially in a hostile position, they should protect themselves by all means. I am a private citizen, and if someone had a gun about to point it at my family or me and I have a gun, of course, I am going to shoot them. But what I am talking about is the instances where there is no weapon or they perceived an object for a weapon, most of the objects do not even resemble a gun, yet they will put multiple bullets in a victim. If you fire your gun and there is no gun present on the suspect, then charges should be filed automatically. That will stop the I Thought I Saw A Gun/Weapon excuse. Also, it would not be so bad if they injured or wounded the suspect, but they are killing them.

Excessive force should be a charge of its own, because if officers empty their clip on someone without a weapon, how can that be justified in court? How many officers will say, when asked in court, why did you fire so many rounds? Well, I thought I was missing them? None. Cops go to gun ranges, just like soldiers, and they know where to aim to kill and I am sure they know where to aim if they just wish to injure someone. In these incidents, if these officers had not killed the suspect, at least they would not be facing murder charges and the suspect lives and has their day in court. NO FUNERALS. And entire concept of a chokehold needs to be banished, because taking someone's life with your bare hands or any submission move is crazy and inhumane.

If someone says, I CAN'T BREATHE!!! Do they believe the suspect is lying? That should be the point where you ease up and ensure the suspect can get some oxygen. That one, I do not understand and do not think I will ever understand. Real head scratcher. Another head scratcher is the fact that we live in the age of technology. So how is it not in the back of a police officer's mind anytime they engage with a suspect with body cam, dash cam and cell phones present, you would think they would be a lot more vigilant. If you are an officer, how many times do you have to see a video of another officer(s) being filmed

doing something that is totally wrong? Yet, somewhere else across America, another

officer is filmed doing something even worst.

If you are a police officer and in the back of your mind something is not saying to you

that you are being filmed or watched, then that is your first problem. If the actions you

take, does not or will not look good on camera, then you may want to take a different

action. As I stated earlier, a career in law enforcement is one I know I could not do, and I

take my hat off to those that do it. However, those that do it, chose to do it, so if you

choose to do something, do it right because you are not only representing yourself, but you

represent everyone that wears the uniform and carries the badge. The bad actions, which

now are being caught on camera, of a few officers are making it harder for everyone else

that wears the uniform and carry the badge. Most people in the communities know who the

good officers, are and who are the corrupt officers. Listen to your communities, that would

be an excellent place to start.

Another Random Thought

Think about how many bad actions (killings, framings, and harassments), that are not recorded and some not even reported or acknowledged over the years. Now, that is scary and crazy at the same time because we all know it to be true. Very few bad, illegal encounters were captured or reported before the year 2000, and it took until recently, that most of them are being captured regularly. Now back to my solution, I think police chiefs, police unions and politicians should make officers aware and let them know that any instance, especially those that cause injury or loss of life will be reviewed immediately.

With video evidence, the review should not take months but a week or two for the district attorney to press charges. Pressing charges does not mean someone is guilty but they did something that warrants the review and decision of a judge and jury, along with having their choice of representation to defend their actions. I understand that no police department wants bad publicity. Still, it always better to get in front of something and take action before it surfaces to light, because the publicity will look and sound a lot worst when

it surfaces days, weeks or even months later. Then it looks as if they were trying to cover it

up or wish it away. The goal is simple, weed out the bad officers and make all the other

officers aware of their actions at all times.

The people in America and in most countries pay the police's salaries, usually through

taxes. So, if there is a group of people that help pay your salary, yet they feel threatened or

terrified by your presence. You have created a negative image on that group within your

society that needs to be addressed. Training should consist of being conscious that you are

always being watched so act like it. Next psychological evaluations should be conducted on

an semi-annual basis, to ensure officers are mentally stable to handle the various situation

they will encounter as a police officer. Then they need to learn to shoot, qualify, and know

if they must discharge their weapon, killing a suspect without a weapon is unlawful. Shoot

to wound, not kill.

There should be some type of simulation program, that lets law enforcement officials

gauge how each officer will react in the various scenarios they may encounter. The simulation should grade the officers, point out mistakes and make suggestions in areas

where they need to improve. It should also let them know if an officer's decisions in the

simulation warrants that they should not be out on the streets policing because they have

demonstrated multiple instances of bad judgment. Sorry, just a random thought.

Back to Politics

I am sorry these random thoughts pop-up, but I have to get them out before I forget, back to these political systems. These gangs/parties exist all over the globe. I have traveled to several countries, and they may go by different names, but you must decide which one you like the best. I chose the United States because most countries I have visited seem to cover one or more stories about the United States and what is going on in its politics. However, they exist in most countries, and they proclaim to do what is best for society/the people, but honestly, who believes a politician one hundred percent of the time. In the west, they vote on so many issues, and most voting happens when the rest of society is either sleeping or not paying attention. Most individuals have no idea about most of the legislations that get passed or rejected. Only the ones that are really significant get coverage, like Brexit or funding the budget or when society gets aggravated and frustrated with something, then they hold these emergency hearing to try and calm down the masses. And this is the political system in your so-called civil societies.

I have visited some other countries, where corruption is not really hidden, it is more like

what can any of you do about it. In the west I would say you would need to be a Sherlock

Holmes type of person, with the time and resources to dig out the corruption. Still, most of

society knows these campaigns do not get funded by good faith and morals alone. If it is

not obvious, the rest of society will carry on with business as usual. I have visited some

countries in Africa where presidents steal from an entire country and go into exile, or they

will have a candidate running for president, but they are in exile, in fear that the current

president will lock them up or cause harm to them. I have heard or witness some

Americans express their displeasure with President Trump, but honestly, I have been in

some countries and heard some stories of their presidents that makes Trump look like a

saint.

In a lot of the impoverished, undeveloped countries, if you do a deep dive into their

politics, well not even a deep dive, just scratch the surface, and if you have any ethics or

morals, it will blow your mind, with the level of corruption and greed. I am going to leave

that there. My mind is tired of the political rant and you get the gist of it all hopefully. The moral of the story, divide them up, make them choose a side, then make them fear what the

other side is trying to do, so they do not see what is really being done. Next ……

Religion

Here we go, another topic that I choose not to discuss with people, not even my family.

I grew up in a deeply religious family and most of my family are still deeply religious.

Once again, I will tread lightly, however these are my thoughts. First, let us agree before

we disagree. There are a lot of religions in the world. We can agree on that. Now for the

disagreement, which religion is the sole true religion? Now the fight begins. Before I go

any further, I just thought of the movie "The Book of Eli." It was a great movie, but the

concept is more real and even better. The guy wanted to get his hand on a Bible because,

with it, he felt he could control the masses. Sounds familiar. Now I am not going to tell

you that I am against any religion, because I am not. To be honest, most people need it,

because it gives them something to believe in and it keeps a lot of people from doing some

evil things, kind of, or shall I say some people. Just because you did not kill anyone, but

you stole from a lot of people or harm a lot of people to benefit yourself or a few people, you are just as bad as the killers and rapist. The worst thing is the people have to live

everyday with what you did to them without anyone getting in trouble from the harm you

have caused. Plus, they will never recover or be repaid what was taken. But back to

religions, can we agree that the most centralized figure in most religions is God and/or the

many names it can go by? Whether it is Brahma, God, Allah, Yahwah, etc. You get the

point, that there is a key figure, essence, or presence that created everything. I agree with

all of you in saying, I believe there is one who created our existence, the universes, the

stars, and everything down to the ants on the ground. I am not going to give it a name

because I do not want to offend any religion at this point, but I am aware of its presence,

and I even have regular conversations with that presences. I say it because no one knows if

it is male, or female, and honestly, it does not matter because, to me, it is the All and its

presence is in every living thing. So now for the disconnect. Who is the true messenger of

that ever so present being and what do those messengers say? Now the war begins. From

this one question, do your research, but throughout history, a lot of people have died, and

wars have been fought over this one question. To be honest, who knows the truth other than the one true presence/being/energy/source or fill in the blank that governs the

universe? Every religion has their scripts, texts, rules, commandments, and most were

written by other men, many years ago, that says it was given to them by the Most Highest.

Correct?

NEW FLASH- (THIS IS NOT TO OFFEND ANYONE)

However, your religion was already decided when you were born, because of where you were born and/or because of the parents that had you. Now, I got that out the way, so what do I mean. Depending on what country or region, you will most likely belong to that religion. The religion your parents' worship will most likely be the religion you follow also. You did not choose what you believe, or what religion you follow. That is my point and you know what, you do not question it either. It is what it is. Just obey the teaching and follow the rules set forth by that religion you are taught to obey, and you will make it to paradise. That sums up most religions in a nutshell. Not really, but sort of. Now we will go deeper into my mind. Two people were created. That is what the main religions believe. But you have some, that believe, all or some of us were created by aliens, but I am not touching on that. So, two people were created. They had to be male and female in order to reproduce. So again, two people (male and female) and the Creator. So how, today we have one planet full of different religions and beliefs. This is where I scratch my head, as a matter of fact, I am getting a headache. It almost made me take a break, but this is

where I need help, because I want to be right like everyone else.

    However, Christianity has how many denominations? Catholics, Presbyterian, Baptist,

Lutheran, Methodist, you get the point. Muslims have two major practices, they do not

care for Christian, and they cannot stand the Jews. Then they do not get along with each

other, besides on the first two things I just mentioned. The Hindu religion has a caste

system, so not only is your religion chosen for you, but the religion decides your place in

society. Siddhartha Gautama founded Buddhism. Now, other than what I was told and/or

taught to believe, how can one be sure which one is right or wrong. Because of belief and

faith, correct? However, I could have been Muslim, Jewish, a Christian you name it,

because it only depended on who my parents are and/or where I was born. By an act of

spiritual randomness or some would say preordained, our religion, our race, our parents,

where we were born and how we look, were already selected for us. Then we get adjusted

to the new surroundings and you start learning new things. Being taught new things and that is what shapes you. Then you become a certain age, where your body and vehicle are all yours. Whatever you want to do with it, you can, because it's yours.

MY QUESTIONS TO YOU: What are you doing with your body/vehicle? Are you an asset or a liability? Are you actually helping to unite the world/planet? Or are you really just pretending you are? Is your body/vehicle causing harm and chaos? Or yet worst, is your body/vehicle only purpose is to harm someone else's body/vehicle. Bringing harm to someone who had no choice, no opinion about where they are born. What religion, race, language or what gender they are. Yet, that's the stuff we fight over. The stuff that makes it a them against us. For some, people they think the fight is the only reason they are here. Tell me that not sad. There are bodies/vehicles who think their only reason is to fight someone else and harm someone else. Destroy nations, instead of uniting a planet. As I said, I want to be right when the time comes, and it could happen come soon if I decide to publish this journey through my mind.

Okay, now I want to share something that was a real headscratcher. I came across this documentary called Life After Life*, and there were these people that had actually died or at least pronounced dead and they crossed over. The shocker is they came back to life and were telling the story of how it was and what they saw. LET'S SAY FOR ME, THAT WAS A GAME CHANGER!!!! People that came back alive and telling what it was like to be dead. I am not going to tell you the whole documentary, because I do not remember it all. But I do remember them all saying, they floated away, and they looked down upon their body. They said they remember being in the presence of a light and that the light was so gentle and loving. When they left, the pain went away, but when they returned to their bodies, they could feel the pain again. ANOTHER GAME CHANGER!!!

The first thing that came to my mind after seeing that, was we are down here discriminating over race, religion, you name it and when you die, if you are living right, because none of the people interviewed seemed to be bad person and they did not seem to be part of the same religion. I'm just going to leave that right there. ANOTHER GAME CHANGER!!!! I happened to run across another documentary about a little boy who remembers dying as an airplane pilot in the early or mid-1900s. He recalls various parts of his past life so vivid that his parents started researching his story. The verdict, his story was totally from his friends to how he died. You can see where I am going with this, but these

are engraved in my mind permanently and sent me on a search, which leads me to where I

am at currently. Grant it, I have seen documentaries of possessed people and they all

looked real, so I will say I believe that stuff too. Then again, I will say this also, I have

seen some UFO and alien documentaries they also look real.

Random Thought

If I see a spaceship/UFO or I just happened to get sucked up into one, because some people have claimed it has happened to them and I'm not saying they are lying, because if it did happened to me, I would hope people or at least someone would believe me. Now, back to my point, if it happens to me, if I can remember because I will definitely be a little scared or even a lot scared, but my question would be. Who do you all worship? Because if you all are hopping from planet to planet and across galaxies, then you and whoever you worship is for real. If a religious person approaches me, I will tell them my story and tell them the Greys, the Martians, whoever, whatever you want to call them, this is who, they worship and I decided to worship who they worship. Hey, you can call me crazy or whatever else. Everyone has had something crazy to go through their mind, so this is mine. THEY HOP PLANETS AND GALAXIES!!! Most people have never left their country, their state and some their village or city. Think about it.

Sorry Back to Religion

Back on religion, but now my mind has nothing else to say on the matter. I think I have said enough, and I hope my thoughts do not get me into any trouble. Speaking on that note, I hope none of my random thoughts get me into any trouble. But, my final thought on religion. How did we created a world of divisions where a planet that is divided and, in the end, our true self/essence/soul floats away and looks down upon a body that went through so much. Fought so hard for or against a race, a religion, a piece of land or whatever else you can name, that we are constantly fighting over. In the end, you look at the body that people will mourn over and let us hope that body/person/soul did some good things to make this world better and not add to the madness. Because I did not say everyone goes or went to the light. Honestly, I cannot remember. You are in my mind, so let me play with yours for once.

Conclusion- What do I think or believe I guess

I know you all have been reading my opinions and my views throughout, yet I have not

quite stated what I think and how I go about this life. Before I say another word, this is not

in any way, how I think or believe someone else must live their life. Your life is your life,

live as one wants to live. Now here is what I think. Most of you are reading this either

have a car, and if not, you know what a car or vehicle is. If someone jumps in their car,

have they now become the car? Anyone that needs an answer to that, I will tell you the

answer is no. They are in the car and controlling it, but they are not a car. Now a person

gets in their car and decides to run into a tree or another car. The person may or may not

be injured but one thing for sure, the vehicle is damaged.

Now that same person decides to use that car and deliver goods, provide a ride for

someone, even rescue someone in need, all which are good things. I think our bodies are,

are vehicles, except we do not get to choose our vehicle. You do not get to choose the make, model or year of our vehicle, but just know we all have a vehicle. Inside that vehicle

is our soul, and I think the soul can guide the vehicle, but it cannot control it. It is in there

for the ride and experiences. I think the soul can guide someone to their passions in life

and helping them choose a career or guide them in making certain decisions, at times.

Now, with that being said, going back to the make and model of your vehicle, how you

act, who you are, your religion, your race and nationality was already chosen for you when

arrived. The parents that raise you, the environment/country you are raised in and the

moral and ethical values taught to you growing up, is what shapes and makes your vehicle.

Your language, religion and in some instances, what and/or who you like, or dislike is

chosen. You figure a child is born and that child has no knowledge of anything.

Everything the child is exposed to growing up, makes and shape that adult. Yet, there is a

soul in there, that was there from the beginning also and that soul is going through that

same experience.

Now, what you do with your vehicle/body is totally up to you once you reach an adult in

most countries. Do you use it for good or do you use it for bad? I think our actions in life does have an effect on our soul. Let me remind you that these are my thoughts, so do not

judge me because, I am not judging you. So why do I call our bodies a vehicle? I think

most people's religion teaches that when the body dies, the soul lives on. So, we should be

able to agree on that. I see the soul as are true being or essence that tries to guide as much

as it can, however as the saying goes, that person has a mind of their own. I believe people

who do bad and evil things, it comes from their mind and not their soul. A bad person's

mind and how they think and the things they do is just a person lost or caught up in the

world/planet. A world or planet that in the year 2020, was mostly built and carved by

generations of dividing the masses and conquering those that are different from us.

Currently, we play nice and talk polite, but we are still labeled and often referred to by

our differences, even though when we die, there is no real difference. I believe it is how

you treat others, that has the greatest impact of the soul and I have my reason for saying

that. Before I go further, I am not saying you should not love yourself, because it all starts

with the love of self. I do not think you can love another if you do not first love yourself.

In my life, I choose to experience some things personally, that I would not have recommended for anyone else try. It was a decision I made for me and it did not affect

anyone else but me. Those types of decisions, I feel, do not carry negative impact on the

soul, because I did not harm anyone. For example, if want to drink some alcohol alone, I

am not harming anyone, but I am personally causing harm to myself, because too much

alcohol does harm to the body and organs. That is the harm I am referring to. I will not say

it has no impact but not a huge, negative impact on the soul. Now, if the harm you cause to

yourself, causes you to harm someone else, I believe that will tremendously impact the

soul. Being that you had a negative impact to someone else's vehicle/body and their soul.

In many instances today, people are hurting and killing other people's vehicle.

    That is why I believe it is how you treat and interact with others is what truly matters.

Grant it, that does not mean it is okay to really hurt or destroy your vehicle either.

Honestly, that will be the last thing the soul will remember and experience before floating

or sinking away. So that will have to be a devastating impact on the soul, as it goes to

____________. You can fill in the blank, not falling for that one. However, it is hard to

believe that a child, with childlike thoughts, can be taught certain things and goes through different experiences. Whether negative or positive, they can grow up to be an adult that

get enjoyment on hurting, killing, stealing from people or thrives on helping others and the

planet. If you have a thought process to where you think or feel that hurting, harming,

manipulating or any form deceit that can cause harm, to a person, a group, a nation or any

of the various forms we separate ourselves from one another, brings pleasure to you, then I

believe it will have a huge negative impact on your soul, and it will have to carry a lot of

that weight. I believe it truly simple, be kind to others, treat them as an extension to

yourself or treat them as if they were you. That way, you will not cause or want to cause

harm to them. In a nutshell, let us go through our life with the intentions of hurting no one,

while enjoying the great things that have been provided to us while on this planet.

The Creator has provided us with a beautiful planet, and we all should strived to do

good, by the Creator and by the planet we live on. Honestly, I could have spewed on with

what I think and how we need to love each other and live as one, but my head hurts and so

do my fingers. I said I was going to complete this book in a day, but it took me two days to

write it. But if you combined the exact times I spent, because I am human, it took about 14 hours, and it only took that long because the idea came to my while I was drinking, so it

started inside of a mind on alcohol. When I read what I had wrote the next day, I

understood would I was trying to say but it was not quite saying it. Anyways, if you are

wondering if it was possible to live as one and do good for one another, check out a

documentary I saw years ago called Thrive. Remarkably interesting. NOW GET OUT MY

HEAD. Good day mate!

Zeek

References

Hughes, A., & Hughes, A. (Directors), Silver, J., & Washington, D. (Producers), & Whitta, G. (Writer). (2010). The book of Eli [Motion picture]. United States: Warner Bros.

Moody, R. A. (2015). Life after life. New York, NY: HarperOne, an imprint of HarperCollins.

 The Case of James Leininger: An American Case of the Reincarnation Type. Explore, 12(3), 200-207. doi:10.1016/j.explore.2016.02.003

www.ingramcontent.com/pod-product-compliance
Lightning Source LLC
Chambersburg PA
CBHW081431250726
48654CB00013B/1920